D0938156

ANCIENT TECHNOLOGY

ANCIENT
CONSTRUCTION

ANCIENT TECHNOLOGY

ANCIENT CONSTRUCTION

FROM TENTS TO TOWERS

by Michael Woods
and
Mary B. Woods

RP RUNESTONE PRESS • MINNEAPOLIS
A DIVISION OF LERNER PUBLISHING GROUP

Dedicated to Phil and Lucy Henshaw, Charlie and Adrienne Burch, George and Bette Mehalko, Hank and Peggy Tufts, Ed and Gisela Sylvester, Bob and Gladys Dennison, Bob and Gail Meighan, John and Anne Kress, and the rest of our Ravenwood Park Friends.

Series designer: Zachary Marell
Series editors: Joelle E. Riley and Dina Drits
Line editor: Margaret J. Goldstein

Runestone Press
A division of Lerner Publishing Group
241 First Avenue North
Minneapolis, MN 55401 U.S.A.

Website address: www.lernerbooks.com

LIBRARY OF CONGRESS CATALOGING-IN-PUBLICATION DATA

Woods, Michael, 1946–
    Ancient Construction: From Tents to Towers / by
Michael and Mary B. Woods.
        p.   cm. — (Ancient technology)
    Includes bibliographical references and index.
    Summary: Describes buildings and structures and examines methods and tools of construction in various civilizations around the world, from prehistoric times up until the end of the Roman Empire.
    ISBN 0–8225–2998–X (lib. bdg. : alk. paper)
    1. Civil engineering—History—to 500 Juvenile literature.
2. Building—History—to 500 Juvenile literature. [1. Civil engineering—History—to 500. 2. Building—History—To 500.]
I. Woods, Michael, 1946–   II. Title. III. Series.
TA149.W64 2000
624'.093—dc21   99-39828

Manufactured in the United States of America
1 2 3 4 5 6 – AM – 05 04 03 02 01 00

TABLE OF CONTENTS

What do you think of when you hear the word *technology*? You probably think of something totally new. You might think of research laboratories filled with computers, powerful microscopes, and other scientific tools. But technology doesn't mean just brand-new machines and discoveries. Technology is as old as human civilization.

Technology is the use of knowledge, inventions, and discoveries to make life better. The word *technology* comes from two Greek words. One, *tekhne*, means "art" or "craft." The other, *logos*, means "logic" or "reason." In Ancient Greece, the word *technology* meant a discussion of arts and crafts. But in modern times, *technology* usually refers to the craft, technique, or tool itself.

People use many kinds of technology. Transportation is one kind of technology. Medicine and agriculture are also kinds of technology. These technologies and many others make life easier, safer, and more enjoyable. This book looks at a form of technology that fulfills the basic human need for shelter: construction.

The story of construction is the story of civilization. The first humans moved from place to place, often building new shelters every time they moved. About ten thousand years ago, humans began to settle into villages and cities. As civilizations grew, people needed larger, more permanent buildings. Construction technology became more sophisticated.

In addition to homes, ancient people built monuments, palaces, roads, dams, bridges, canals, tunnels, harbors, lighthouses, sewage systems, and many other structures. Ancient builders, architects, engineers, plumbers, carpenters, and masons all worked to build structures that looked good and were suitable for specific uses.

ANCIENT ROOTS

You've probably heard people remark, "There's nothing new under the sun!" That's an exaggeration, of course. Yet there's much truth in the saying when we're talking about construction. Ancient people developed most of our modern building materials, including concrete, glass, bricks, and tiles.

The word *ancient* refers to the time period beginning with the first humans on earth and ending with the fall of the Western Roman Empire in A.D. 476. The first humans lived about 2.5 million years ago. Technology is one trait that historians and scientists use to distinguish ancient humans from their prehuman ancestors.

The first construction technology was primitive. Early humans used poles and animal skins to make tents. They wove reeds together and plastered them with mud to make huts. A tree trunk laid across a stream was the first bridge. Mud packed into molds and dried in the sun made the first bricks. These techniques were simple, yet they were effective.

CIVILIZATIONS OF THE
Ancient World
(through A.D. 476)

EUROPE

ASIA

AFRICA

Indian Ocean

6000 B.C. ——————————— 534 B.C.	Middle East
3100 B.C. ——————— 30 B.C.	Egypt
1766 B.C. ———————	China
1200 B.C. ———————	Mesoamerica
800 B.C. ——— 146 B.C.	Greece
509 B.C. ——— A.D. 476	Rome
320 B.C. —	India

Stone Age civilizations have flourished in
most parts of the world. These cultures began and
ended at different times in different regions.

Architecture, the science and art of building, is one aspect of construction. Ancient civilizations often had their own unique architectural styles. Many of these styles resulted from environmental factors. For instance, people living in a warm climate needed buildings with good ventilation. People in cold regions needed airtight structures that could be heated.

The building materials themselves depended on the environment. People who lived in the forests of Europe had plenty of timber, so they built structures from wood. Wood was scarce in ancient Egypt, but Egypt had plenty of soft limestone. So the Egyptians built great stone palaces and pyramids. The *Flintstones* cartoon characters would be proud of the construction material used 15,000 years ago in the Ukraine—mammoth tusks and bones covered with animal skins.

Ancient builders developed new materials and technology by trial and error. Sometimes they copied and improved on technology used by other cultures. Later, modern builders copied techniques developed in the ancient world.

It took modern builders centuries to surpass the accomplishments of ancient architects. The dome of the Parthenon in Greece was the world's biggest dome until the nineteenth century. The Great Pyramid at Giza in Egypt was the highest structure in the world for more than four thousand years. Many techniques developed in the ancient world—for roofing buildings, for example—are still used.

This book tells the story of these and other achievements of ancient construction. Read on and discover the wonders of the ancient builders.

THE STONE AGE

Historians call the first period in human society the Stone Age. The first humans, who lived about 2.5 million years ago, were hunters and gatherers. They lived in small groups and got their food by catching game, fishing, and gathering wild plants. When the food in one area was all used up, the group moved to a new place.

Archaeologists, scientists who study the remains of past cultures, think that early humans were skilled in building temporary homes. Early builders used whatever materials were available. They made lean-tos from tree branches propped against cliffs, rocks, or other supports. They made huts of tree branches woven together into frames. They made tents and tepees from poles tied together and covered with animal skins. Some early houses were portable. Tepees, for instance, could be easily taken apart, moved, and rebuilt in a new place.

Archaeologists have found the remains of ancient tent posts that were pounded into the ground. They have also found rocks, arranged in circles, that probably supported wooden tent posts. The posts may have been tied together at the top to form tepees. Animal skins probably covered the frames.

Early homes were probably small, dark, dirty, and smelly. Cooking fires probably filled the insides of huts with smoke and covered everyone with soot. But early people spent very little time inside their dwellings. They were busy most of the day finding and preparing food. They went inside only to sleep or escape bad weather, and they were probably happy to use their simple dwellings when it was time to rest. Although simple, lean-tos, huts, and tents provided shelter from wind, cold, rain, snow, and sun.

FEW CAVEMEN LIVED IN CAVES

Many people think that our ancestors in the Stone Age lived in caves. After all, some people use the term *cavemen* to refer to primitive people. But very few Stone Age people were cave dwellers. Caves didn't make pleasant houses. They were damp and dark. Few caves were big enough for a whole family. Even fewer were located near good supplies of freshwater and game for hunting.

Besides, many caves already had occupants—cave bears, cave lions, and cave hyenas. Imagine trying to move into a cave in Stone Age times. If you chased the animals out, they might come back in the middle of the night. Bats also made their homes in caves. It would have been nasty to share a cave with bats that hung upside down from the ceiling and left droppings all over the floor.

But some early humans, especially in cold places, did live in caves. Because their walls are made of thick layers of earth and stone, caves were sometimes warmer than other Stone Age dwellings. In northern regions and during ice ages—cold periods in earth's history—caves helped keep people from freezing.

One of the oldest cave dwellings is in southern France. There, archaeologists have found remains of fire pits, animal bones, and stone tools, showing that people lived in the cave 500,000 years ago. Another ancient cave dwelling is near Beijing in southern China. People lived there, generation after generation, between 500,000 and 250,000 years ago.

Ancient cave dwellers actually spent most of their time just outside the cave entrance. This was the main living area, where people cooked, made clothing and tools, and slept. People probably retreated into the cave only in bad weather, when enemies approached, or to perform magic.

Cro-Magnon people, who lived in western Asia and Europe about 40,000 years ago, painted beautiful pictures of animals on cave walls. Perhaps the Cro-Magnons believed that caves had magical properties and used them as sacred buildings.

ANCIENT BRIDGES

The world's first bridge builder was the first Stone Age person to cut down a tree so that it dropped across a creek. The banks of the creek supported the bridge on both ends. Later, Stone Age people built longer bridges, with several tree trunks resting on big rocks in a river.

One variation was the clapper bridge, built with big flat pieces of slate or other stones that overlapped to form a walkway. Piles of stone served as piers, or support points,

The construction of the moai (above) on Easter Island and of Stonehenge (facing page) in Wiltshire, England, has puzzled archaeologists for centuries.

beneath the walkway. The word *clapper* comes from a Latin term, *claperius*, meaning "pile of stones."

Ancient people even built suspension bridges. They used two ropes made from twisted vines to span a river. Shorter ropes, hanging from the main ropes, supported a narrow wooden deck, over which people could walk single file. Modern suspension bridges, like the Golden Gate Bridge in San Francisco, are built in somewhat the same way. But modern suspension bridges have big, woven-steel cables that support the deck.

THE MOAI OF EASTER ISLAND

One island in the world is famous only because of the ancient monuments built there. It is remote Easter Island, located in the South Pacific Ocean, 2,300 miles west of Chile.

Experts think Easter Island was settled around A.D. 400. The islanders built about six hundred huge stone statues, called moai, probably to honor ancestors. The statues are figures of people, some with huge stone slabs on their heads. Most of the moai are 10 to 20 feet high and stand on stone platforms. A few stand 40 feet high and weigh as much as 90 tons. Easter Islanders carved the statues out of soft volcanic rock, probably using stone tools.

During a war on the island in 1680, soldiers knocked the moai down, and most of them broke. But about 15 statues have been restored to their original positions, looking out over the Pacific Ocean.

ANCIENT MYSTERY: STONEHENGE

One of the biggest mysteries of ancient construction is Stonehenge. It is a huge, circular stone monument built by ancient people in Wiltshire, England, between 3000 and 1800 B.C. Archaeologists have had to guess at the original appearance of the monument, because over the centuries, some stones have fallen down, and people have carted stones away to build dams, bridges, and other structures.

Archaeologists believe that the original monument was surrounded by a circular ditch and a wall of piled earth and stone, 320 feet in diameter. Inside stood large blocks of gray sandstone, arranged in a circle. Each block was about 13 feet high and weighed about 28 tons! Smaller stone slabs were laid on top of the blocks, connecting the whole circle. Inside was another circle, made of smaller blue stones, each weighing up to four tons. In the middle, two horseshoe-shaped sets of stones formed an entrance.

Experts believe that Stonehenge was an astronomical observatory, connected in some way with sun worship. A big, flat sandstone block, about 60 feet long, formed an altar. A marker stone to the east was positioned to cast a shadow on the altar on June 21, the summer solstice, or first day of summer.

We know little about how Stonehenge was built. People probably dug up earth to create the outer wall using bones, stones, antlers, and their bare hands. Some of the blue stones came from a place 240 miles away from Stonehenge. Archaeologists estimate that dragging just one stone to the site would have involved five hundred people.

How did they lift the stones? Who designed Stonehenge? Who built it? Why? Nobody knows the answers, and Stonehenge remains one of the most mysterious of all ancient structures.

ANCIENT MIDDLE EAST

An Assyrian relief depicts a creature with the body of a bull, wings, and a human face.

Between 10,000 and 3500 B.C., ancient people began abandoning the hunter-gatherer lifestyle and became more settled. In the ancient Middle East, in a rich growing region called the Fertile Crescent, people began to farm the land and build permanent villages. One group settled between the Tigris and Euphrates Rivers in the modern country of Iraq. The region was later named Mesopotamia, which means "between rivers."

Some of our most important construction technology originated in the ancient Middle East. This technology includes building materials such as bricks and mortar, techniques like town planning, and structures such as toilets, sewers, and permanent houses. In fact, the world's first permanent dwellings were built in Mesopotamia about nine thousand years ago.

MUD AND WATTLE

No, mud and wattle was not a popular dance in the ancient Middle East. Mud and wattle was one of the first and most widely used techniques for making homes. The building process began with a simple frame, made from long, thin poles or reeds. Ancient builders often used a plant called the giant reed, which can grow to be 18 feet tall.

The reeds or poles were woven together to produce a strong skeleton, called a wattle work. The wattle work was then plastered with mud or clay, which hardened in the sun. Mud-and-wattle construction made snug homes that held up for years in places that didn't get much rain. People in some poor countries still build mud-and-wattle huts.

BRICK BY BRICK

Mesopotamia had plenty of clay and mud, which lined the banks of the Tigris and Euphrates Rivers. At first the Mesopotamians built whole walls from packed mud and clay. Then they began to pack mud into four-sided wooden frames. The mud dried to create uniform bricks that could be stacked to make straight, even walls. Archaeologists know that sun-dried bricks were used in Ur, a Mesopotamian city, in about 4000 B.C.

Eventually builders realized that mixing chopped straw with mud or clay made bricks stronger. Straw also kept mud and clay from cracking as bricks dried in the hot sun. Brick, of course, is still one of our most important building materials.

ONE THING LEADS TO ANOTHER

Sometimes a breakthrough in one area of technology provides unexpected benefits in another area. For instance, pottery making in ancient Mesopotamia had a positive

The Mesopotamians used bricks to build ziggurats (stepped pyramids), such as this one from the eleventh century B.C.

effect on brick making. The first pottery bowls and jugs were made from sun-dried clay. But they broke easily and sometimes leaked. Then a pottery maker discovered that firing pottery—heating it in an oven—made it much harder, stronger, and more water resistant than sun-dried

Detail from a wall in Babylon made of glazed ceramic brick

pottery. In fact, pottery heated in an oven became as hard as stone.

Pottery makers then learned to make a hard glaze—a glasslike coating—by melting sand and other minerals onto the surface of pottery during firing. Glazes made pottery even harder and more waterproof.

Brick makers borrowed this technology. Around 3000 B.C., they began to fire bricks. Fired bricks, like fired pottery, were hard and water resistant. Next, brick makers made glazed bricks, with the same kind of waterproof, glasslike coating used on pottery.

BETTER ROOFS

Many of the first ancient houses had thatched roofs, which were made of straw, leaves, or branches bundled together. Thatch shed water well, keeping people dry during rainy weather. But thatch couldn't keep out stinging and blood-sucking insects. It had to be replaced every few years—which meant taking the whole roof off the house. Thatch also caught on fire easily.

Because of the thatched roof's drawbacks, the development of clay roofing tiles was a great advance in building technology. The advance happened in Mesopotamia. Clay tiles, fired like pottery, were longer lasting and more waterproof than thatch. Whereas thatched roofs had to be steeply sloped, so that rain would run off quickly and not leak into houses, tiled roofs did not. The development of roofing tiles led to the creation of beautiful buildings, such as classic Greek temples with low-pitched roofs.

A BUILDING MATERIAL FROM HELL

Parts of the Middle East have big underground deposits of petroleum, or crude oil. In modern times, people use petroleum to make many products, including gasoline and asphalt. People in Mesopotamia used petroleum too.

One by-product of petroleum is bitumen, which oozes out of the ground, sits in pools, and hardens in the hot sun. The Mesopotamians thought that bitumen came from a lake in the "underground," a hellish region that was home to evil spirits. But the fear of evil spirits didn't stop ancient people from collecting bitumen. They gathered it from the ground and from the Dead Sea, where it seeped from the seafloor, hardened, and floated on the surface of the water in huge strands. The modern town of Hit, about 90 miles west of present-day Baghdad in Iraq, was named for its main product, bitumen.

Bitumen was used as a strong, waterproof mortar between bricks and as a waterproof coating for walls, sewers, irrigation ditches—even ships. Builders first melted the bitumen to drive off any water it contained, then they mixed it with substances such as sand, chopped reeds, straw, and powdered limestone. These fillers added thickness, so the mixture didn't run off when it was applied to a wall or other surface, and made the mortar stronger. Bitumen was processed right at construction sites and was used immediately while still hot.

They Beat Ol' Tom Crapper

Some people think that Thomas Crapper, an English plumber, invented the toilet in the 1860s—and gave it the slang name "crapper." But historians disagree. They point out that another English plumber, Albert Giblin, patented a toilet in 1819. Actually, though, the Mesopotamians beat out both of these men by inventing toilets thousands of years earlier.

Mesopotamian toilets were low walls of hardened brick with open seats on top. Toilet floors were coated with bitumen and opened into sewer pipes—rings of fired clay, also sealed with bitumen. Some Mesopotamian palaces had several toilets lined up side by side.

Toilets and sewers were great advances in construction technology. They helped prevent the spread of disease and made city life more pleasant. In fact, many ancient cities were cleaner, healthier places than major European cities of the seventeenth, eighteenth, and early nineteenth centuries—when human wastes were often simply dumped into the street.

Ancient Town Planning

Some cities develop naturally—almost helter-skelter—as the population grows. It's easy to recognize an unplanned town. The streets may be narrow and crooked, running every which way with no logical order. The city may have few parks or open areas in which people can relax.

Other towns are planned. They tend to have broad, straight streets that intersect at right angles, plenty of parks and public squares, and an atmosphere of order. In some cities, planners figure out how many movie theaters, shopping centers, and gas stations will be allowed. They might even determine the style and size of buildings. Some cities, such as Celebration, Florida, are completely planned from scratch.

Town planning might sound like a modern idea, but it actually began in ancient times. Babylon, the most famous ancient Middle Eastern city, did not begin as a planned town. But as Babylon grew, houses and roads were built according to a definite plan. Here's how the Greek historian Herodotus described the city's orderly appearance:

> It lies on a great plain, and is in the shape of a square, each side an hundred and twenty furlongs in length; thus 480 furlongs make the complete circuit of the city... they built houses, of a single chamber, facing each other, with space enough for the driving of a four-horse chariot.... There are an hundred gates in the circle of the wall, all of bronze, with posts and lintels of the same kind.

A re-creation of the Ishtar Gate, which once protected the city of Babylon, is located at the Iraq Museum in Baghdad.

BUILDING TO SURVIVE

Ancient town planners tried to design cities that could be protected from enemy attacks. For instance, important buildings were placed on top of hills, because hills were easily defended. Many ancient towns were also surrounded by high walls with strong gates.

The first city walls were simple structures made from heaps of stone and earth. But builders soon developed great skill in making better fortifications out of brick and stone. One Mesopotamian city was protected by two walls, each of which was three hundred feet high. Each wall was wide enough at the top for six chariots to drive side by side, fighting off attackers.

The entrance gate was often the weakest spot in a city wall. So builders took special care to make gates strong and difficult to penetrate. At one Mesopotamian fortress, built around 3100 B.C., brick walls lined the road that led to the entrance gate. The road narrowed as it approached the gate—a design that forced attackers to crowd tightly together as they rushed toward the gate. Right at the entrance, defenders in high towers could throw rocks, spears, burning oil, and other objects down on the crowded attackers.

TOWNS WITH TERRACES

Many Mesopotamian towns included terraces, raised mounds of earth or ledges cut into hillsides that resemble the layers on a wedding cake. Terraces were often planted with fruit trees and flowers. Some terraces even had buildings on top. The famous Hanging Gardens of Babylon, one of the Seven Wonders of the Ancient World, were said to have been built on terraces.

To hold the tons of soil and any buildings that might be erected there, terraces needed strong supporting walls. The walls had to be several feet thick and made from brick or stone. Without supporting walls, the terraces would have collapsed.

Ancient Wonders: Part 1

The "Seven Wonders of the Ancient World" were the most impressive structures of ancient times. The wonders were monuments to gods, palaces for kings, and other structures that seemed fantastic beyond belief. They were also monuments to the skill of ancient builders.

The Greek historian Herodotus made the first list of wonders in the fifth century B.C. Other lists have been drawn up over the centuries. According to Herodotus, the wonders were the Hanging Gardens of Babylon, the Mausoleum at Halicarnassus, the Great Pyramid at Giza, the Statue of Zeus at Olympia, the Temple of Artemis at Ephesus, the Colossus of Rhodes, and the Pharos of Alexandria.

Only one of Herodotus's Seven Wonders, the Great Pyramid at Giza, has survived to modern times. So experts can only guess at the true size and appearance of the other structures.

The Hanging Gardens of Babylon: The Hanging Gardens of Babylon surrounded a hillside palace built by King Nebuchadrezzar II in the sixth century B.C. The gardens were planted on terraces—ledges cut into the hillside—and they seemed to hang, suspended in space, from the sides of the palace.

The gardens held a fantastic assortment of palm trees, fruiting plants, and flowers. Exotic birds and animals lived among the plants, and sunlight glittered off many waterfalls on the hillside. Nebuchadrezzar was said to have built the gardens as a gift for his sweetheart, who was homesick for the mountainous countryside of her childhood.

The gardens stood on the eastern bank of the Euphrates River, about 30 miles south of modern Baghdad. The builders created irrigation canals to bring river water to the garden plants. We know very little else about the gardens or how they were built. In fact, some archaeologists think the gardens never existed and are just a beautiful legend.

The Mausoleum at Halicarnassus: The Mausoleum at Halicarnassus was a tomb built for King Mausolus, an ancient Persian ruler. Completed around 350 B.C., the tomb measured 120 by 100 feet at its base and rose to a height of 140 feet. It contained a polished stone burial chamber topped by statues and a pyramid-shaped roof. At the very top of the roof, archaeologists believe, were statues of King Mausolus and his queen, riding in a chariot pulled by four horses.

The tomb remained intact for more than 1,600 years, until it was badly damaged by an earthquake. In 1494, the Knights of St. John, crusaders who had invaded the area, decided to repair a castle they had built nearby. Where could they find stones? In the tomb, of course. The crusaders took the structure apart, block by block. It was dismantled completely by about 1522. But tourists can still see the castle in Bodrum, in modern-day Turkey, and identify the polished blocks taken from the tomb.

Mausolus's wife built the tomb to be sure that people would remember her husband. Even though the tomb is gone, we have not forgotten Mausolus. Our English word for a large, aboveground tomb is *mausoleum,* named for the king.

It took an amazing amount of work to build terraces. Archaeologists studied one terrace in Mesopotamia and concluded that it contained 14 million tons of earth. Moving that much soil would have required 12,000 men working for 10 years.

WHAT A TUNNEL!

A tunnel is a horizontal underground passageway, usually made by digging through soil or rock. In Babylon an impressive brick-lined tunnel connected the city's royal palace and its temple, located more than half a mile apart on opposite sides of the Euphrates River. The tunnel allowed pedestrians—people on foot—to cross under the river.

Builders started digging the tunnel around 2180 B.C. and finished 20 years later. Archaeologists believe that builders worked during the dry season, when the river was very low. Bitumen was used to waterproof the brick chamber.

ANCIENT EGYPT

In this Egyptian painting, a surveyor takes measurements with a rope.

Ancient Egypt is famous for its great construction projects. The Egyptians believed their pharaohs, or kings, were gods, so enormous palaces, monuments, and tombs were built to honor them. Pharaohs wanted to emphasize their great power, and they encouraged architects to build massive, overpowering monuments.

The country had huge deposits of limestone, a relatively soft rock that could be cut with the copper chisels, saws, and other tools used in ancient Egypt. Would the Egyptians have built giant pyramids if they had had only granite, a much harder rock? Probably not. Granite is so hard that it would have bent the Egyptians' copper tools.

FIRST ARCHITECT...FIRST ENGINEER...FIRST PYRAMID

An Egyptian man named Imhotep was the first engineer and the first architect recorded in history. He created the pyramid design that made ancient Egypt so famous. He designed the first pyramid built in Egypt—and probably the first in the world. It was the Step Pyramid at Saqqara, built as a tomb for King Djoser in the 2600s B.C. It is the world's oldest remaining stone building.

Imhotep was born around 2650 B.C. in Memphis, near modern-day Cairo. His name means "he who comes in peace." Imhotep was an adviser to King Djoser. He was also an all-round genius—accomplished as an architect, writer, statesman, and even a physician. The Egyptians later worshiped Imhotep as a god of medicine.

Cutting Pyramid Stones

Archaeologists have identified the ruins of at least 70 pyramids along Egypt's Nile River. Three of the most famous were built at Giza, near Cairo, between 2600 and 2500 B.C. These were the tombs of kings Khufu, Khafre, and Menkure. The pyramids were constructed of huge blocks of limestone.

Egyptian stonecutters had a clever way of removing the big blocks of stone from quarries. They worked from the edges and corners, where two or three faces of a stone slab might already be exposed. They cut narrow grooves in the stone or drilled holes along a line where they wanted to cut. Next the stonecutters pounded wooden wedges into the holes or grooves and soaked the wedges with water.

Wood swells and expands when wet, so the wedges swelled and, after about 12 hours, began to crack the rock along the cut line. As the cracks got bigger, the stonecutters inserted larger wedges and repeated the steps until the slab of rock broke free. Stonecutters in other ancient civilizations used the same technology.

Ancient Wonders: Part 2

The Great Pyramid at Giza: Completed around 2560 B.C., the Great Pyramid at Giza is the oldest of the Seven Wonders of the Ancient World and the only one still in existence. The largest of the Egyptian pyramids, it is the tomb of King Khufu.

The Great Pyramid once rose to a height of 481 feet—as tall as a 48-story skyscraper—though some of its upper stones are now gone. Each side of its base is 755 feet long—longer than 2 football fields—and it covers an area bigger than 10 football fields. The pyramid contains more than two million blocks of limestone; most weigh about 3.5 tons—heavier than two cars. Except for the Great Wall of China, the Great Pyramid was the biggest structure in the ancient world. For 4,300 years, until the nineteenth century, it was the tallest building in the world.

The Great Pyramid was built big—but with great precision. The base is almost a perfect square. It is oriented almost exactly in north-south and east-west directions. The limestone blocks fit together so tightly that you can't fit a credit card between them.

The Greek historian Herodotus said that 100,000 men worked for 20 years to build the Great Pyramid. Many of these laborers were farmers, who worked on construction projects when the Nile River flooded their fields in spring. They would have been idle at this time anyway.

Moving Pyramid Stones

The blocks used to build the pyramids weighed two to five tons each. How did workers move such heavy blocks? They first used sledges, or sleds, to pull the blocks from quarries to the Nile River. Using rafts, they floated the blocks down the Nile to construction sites.

How did they lift blocks into place on the pyramid itself? As a pyramid rose higher, experts believe, workers would build an earthen ramp around its sides. The ramp grew higher and higher with each new course of stone. Using sledges, laborers then hauled the big stones up the ramp. When the pyramid was completed, workers tore down the ramp and hauled the dirt away. Archaeologists have identified remains of earthen ramps at several pyramid sites.

Queen Hatshepsut's Temple

One of the most famous temples in ancient Egypt, built for Queen Hatshepsut, was erected at Deir el-Bahri around 1480 B.C. Hatshepsut was married to King Thutmose II, who died around 1504 B.C. Afterward, she ordered herself crowned pharaoh.

Queen Hatshepsut's architect, Senmut, designed the temple to fit in with its environment. He placed the building at the foot of a huge limestone cliff. The temple's limestone walls, columns, and terraces almost seemed like extensions of the cliff itself. Stone ramps rose from one terrace to another, so people could climb to the altar at the top of the temple. On the temple walls, carvings told of the queen's deeds, including a famous trading expedition to the land of Punt on the coast of East Africa.

Queen Hatshepsut's temple blends in with the limestone cliffs.

PRACTICAL CONSTRUCTION

The ancient Egyptians did more than build pyramids, temples, and other monuments. They also built practical structures, including canals and dams. One of the biggest ancient dams, located southwest of modern Cairo, was about 370 feet long, 33 feet high, and 270 feet thick in some places. It was made of limestone blocks and was built to store water for workers in nearby stone quarries.

Around 1300 B.C., Egyptian engineers built an even larger stone dam across the Orontes River in Syria. About 1.25 miles long, the dam held back the river, forming Lake Homs. The dam and the lake still provide water for Syrian farms.

TOILETS FIT FOR A KING

Like the Mesopotamians, the Egyptians built toilets and drains. Some Egyptian toilets were quite elaborate, with copper drainpipes for carrying away waste material. Other toilets were simple stone boxes that had to be emptied by hand. Clay pots were probably placed in the bottom of these toilets to make removing waste easier. Some Egyptian toilets had comfortable wooden seats, but many seats were made from stone—they must have been chilly on cold mornings.

Even pyramids had toilets! The ancient Egyptians believed in an afterlife, so they stocked pyramids with food, clothing, and other items that the dead rulers might need on their journey to the next world. In case the rulers needed to go to the bathroom, the pyramid builders installed toilets inside pyramids and other tombs, beginning about 2500 B.C.

ANCIENT INDIA
AND CHINA

People in the northwestern part of India began settling into villages around 4000 B.C. They built the same kind of mud-and-wattle huts found in early Mesopotamia. Within a thousand years, one of the world's greatest civilizations had emerged in this region. We call it the Indus Valley civilization, because it developed along the Indus River in modern-day Pakistan.

Westerners weren't even aware of the Indus Valley civilization until 1922, when archaeologists found remains of brick buildings and began to explore the area. Eventually archaeologists uncovered remains of more than 50 villages and towns.

At least two large cities ruled the region. One was Mohenjo Daro, located on the Indus River. The other was Harappa, built on a tributary of the Indus about four hundred miles northeast. Archaeologists believe that Mohenjo Daro had a population of 40,000. Harappa may have had 35,000 people.

Modern-day remains of the planned town of Mohenjo Daro

The Indus Valley civilization lasted for about a thousand years, from 3000 to 2000 B.C., then the people abandoned their towns and cities. Historians are not sure why they left.

TOWN PLANNING

Harappa and Mohenjo Daro are among the earliest examples of planned towns. Planners used the same approach for both cities. A huge, brick building—about 40 feet high, 400 yards long, and 200 yards wide—stood in the center of town. Built on a platform of packed earth and stone, the building served as a protective fortress. On top were a grain storehouse, government offices, and other public facilities.

City streets spread out from the fortress in a rectangular pattern that resembled a sheet of graph paper. Streets ran north and south, east and west. The main streets ranged from 9 to 34 feet wide, and some ran straight as an arrow for about half a mile. Homes, shops, and other buildings lined the streets.

Homes had solid walls, with no windows or doors that faced the street. This arrangement gave residents privacy and also helped protect houses from thieves. Doors were located in the backs of the houses, reached by narrow paths behind the main streets. The doors often opened into courtyards, where people probably ate and worked in good weather.

Most of the Indus Valley homes had two stories and were built according to the same plan. Walls were made from big, flat bricks, about 20 by 10 inches and 3.5 inches thick—much larger than modern bricks.

Ancient Indian brick makers stacked clay bricks into mounds that resembled beehives. Then they lit fires underneath the mounds and kept them burning for hours, until the bricks were hardened like pottery. This method allowed brick makers to harden large numbers of bricks all at once.

ANCIENT PLUMBING

Mohenjo Daro and Harappa are known for having some of the ancient world's most advanced toilets and sewers. "No other

A Roman pipe used in plumbing, based on an Indian design

ancient civilization until that of the Romans had so efficient a system of drains," wrote A. L. Basham, an expert on ancient India.

Toilets were probably "flushed" with a pitcher of water after each use. Wastes then traveled down a drainpipe, to underground sewer pipes that drained into the river. This system allowed disease to spread, because people living downstream from the town used the same river for drinking and bathing.

The central fortress at Mohenjo Daro held one of the world's first public baths, a large brick building with dressing rooms and a central courtyard. The courtyard contained a bathing pool, about eight feet deep, with flights of stairs leading right into the water. The pool itself was made from waterproof bricks, made of clay mixed with bitumen. Water from the pool emptied through a drainpipe, also made from waterproof bricks.

ANCIENT SEAPORTS

Seaports are important centers of commerce and transportation. Cargo ships are loaded and unloaded at seaports. Soldiers, merchants, and other people traveling by water depart and arrive at seaports. Seaports need special facilities, such as harbors protected from high waves, docks for loading and unloading cargo, warehouses for storing products, and roads for moving goods in from farms and out to markets.

Many ancient peoples built big port facilities for commercial and military ships. One of the first ancient ports was built at Lothal, an Indian city on the Gulf of Khambhat in the Arabian Sea. From there, Indian ships traveled through the Persian Gulf to ports in Mesopotamia. They carried goods such as barley, wheat, cotton, ivory, gold, and timber for trade.

The shipping facilities at Lothal included a brick dock more than seven hundred feet long. A watertight gate held water from the high tide, so that ships stayed level with the dock at both high and low tides. Thus ships could be loaded and unloaded 24 hours a day.

ANCIENT CHINA

The first villages and cities in China were built along the Yellow River, or Huang Ho, in about 3000 B.C. The Chinese built the same kind of mud-and-wattle huts found in other ancient civilizations.

The first Chinese era described in written records was the Shang dynasty (1766–1122 B.C.). Historians know that the Chinese traded goods with the Mesopotamians during this era. The ancient Chinese and Mesopotamians may have exchanged ideas about construction and other technology as well.

THE SAME BRIGHT IDEA

Throughout history, people in different places have shown an amazing knack for finding similar solutions to technological problems. Often, different groups found the same solution at about the same time, although they were separated by thousands of miles. The development of central heating—a system for warming an entire building from a single source—is one example of people in different places getting the same bright idea.

The first central heating system may have been developed in China during the Han dynasty, between 206 B.C. and A.D. 220. In this simple but effective system, houses were built with a raised stone floor. A fire built in the space beneath the floor heated the whole house.

About a hundred years after the Chinese invented this system, the ancient Romans developed the same basic idea, which they called a hypocaust. With this system, floors were built on pillars, creating a hollow area under each room. Hot air from a furnace located outside a house or building circulated under the floors, warming rooms before escaping through a pipe in the roof. The furnace usually burned charcoal or wood.

The first hyopcausts were used to heat public baths in Rome. Later, they became common in many homes and other structures. Unlike fireplaces, which heated just one room, central heating systems provided steady warmth throughout entire dwellings.

The expansive Great Wall of China

THE GREAT WALL OF CHINA

When astronauts made flights to the moon in the late 1960s, they reported that only one human-made structure on earth was visible from outer space. It was the Great Wall of China, built to protect the Chinese from northern invaders.

The ancient Chinese built walls to protect their borders as early as the 600s B.C. Around 220 B.C., Emperor Shih Huang Ti decided to build a wall all the way across northern China, as protection against Mongolian invaders. Construction took hundreds of years, as workers built new sections of wall and connected them with older protective walls.

Counting all the curves and bends, the wall stretched for more than 2,500 miles—over mountains and through valleys. In terms of size, the wall was the greatest structure ever built in the ancient world. It averaged about 30 feet in height. It was about 25 feet thick at its base and 15 feet wide at the top. A paved road for workers and soldiers ran along the top of the wall. Watchtowers, about 45 feet high, were located about 250 feet apart. Deep ditches were dug along the northern side of the wall as an extra defense against invaders.

Workers built the Great Wall with whatever materials were available near each section. Most of the wall was made from packed soil and stones, covered with a facing of stones or bricks. Stonemasons tried hard to follow a rule set down by Emperor Shih Huang Ti. He wanted all the stone blocks and bricks to fit together exactly. He ordered construction bosses to cut off the head of any worker who left gaps between the blocks!

Most of the original wall collapsed over the centuries. Much of the modern Great Wall was rebuilt from the ruins in the late 1600s.

ANCIENT MESOAMERICA

The name Mesoamerica refers to the ancient civilizations of Mexico and Central America, including the Aztecs, Maya, and Olmec. The Olmec civilization was one of the earliest in Mesoamerica, emerging before 1200 B.C. The Maya began settling into farming villages as early as 1000 B.C. Eventually, Maya towns and cities stretched from southern Mexico through the modern countries of Honduras, Guatemala, and Belize.

Few written records remain from these groups, but excavations reveal that Mesoamerican technology was very advanced. The Maya built large cities with magnificent stone temple-pyramids, palaces, and other structures. One city, Tikal, had a population of 50,000. The Maya used a form of picture-writing and had an advanced knowledge of mathematics.

MYSTERIOUS HEADS

Among the ancient world's most mysterious monuments are giant stone heads carved by the

Olmec. The sculptures stand four and a half to nine feet high and weigh many tons. They have flat faces, thickened lips, and helmetlike hats resembling those worn by modern football players.

The heads were carved from basalt and andesite. The rock came from a quarry located some 50 miles from the sites where the sculptures were placed. Archaeologists don't know how the Olmec moved such heavy blocks of stone that far.

SINGING STAIRWAYS

The Maya city of Chichén Itzá was built in the fifth or sixth century A.D. The city is famous for its huge temple-pyramid. Centuries ago, archaeologists think, the Maya might have conducted bloody ceremonies at the pyramid. With thousands of people gathered around, captives from battle were forced to climb to the top of the pyramid. When each prisoner reached the top, a holy man would slice open his chest with a razor-sharp stone knife and pull out his still-beating heart! Blood flowed down the stairs, over captives who were still climbing.

Visitors to the pyramid have noted that hand-clapping causes the staircases to produce strange, high-pitched echoes. Some scientists believe that the sounds are no accident. Ancient Maya builders may have designed the stairways as acoustic chambers, created to amplify and change sounds. Some scientists think that the builders were trying to reproduce the song of the quetzal, a bird sacred to the Maya. Imagine the spooky sound as a huge crowd watching human sacrifices clapped and yelled, like spectators in a modern football stadium.

A ninety-two-step staircase leads to the top of the Maya pyramid at Chichén Itzá.

DUAL-PURPOSE STRUCTURES

La Milpa was a Maya kingdom located in the rain forest of modern-day Belize. Thousands of Maya lived in La Milpa during the civilization's "Golden Age," which began around A.D. 100. Like many other Maya cities, La Milpa had a huge public square paved with cobblestones. This four-acre square, or Great Plaza, probably served as a marketplace and gathering spot for the Maya. But archaeologists believe that the square was also a key part of the ancient Maya's water supply system.

Although La Milpa was built in a rain forest, the region where the Maya lived had few rivers or other permanent sources of water. Water would have been very scarce during the long dry season, from November to May. How did the Maya get water for their crops and for the thousands of people living in their cities?

Archaeologists think that the Maya designed systems to catch and store water that fell during the rainy season. At La Milpa, for instance, water ran off the cobblestones of the Great Plaza into a series of drainage canals, dams, and reservoirs. The dams and canals were very primitive, built from stone blocks and packed clay. But they were effective at gathering and storing water.

CLEVER DESIGNERS

Maya houses had walls of flat stones layered one on top of another. To make roofs for the houses, Maya builders developed a clever design, called a corbeled roof. With the house walls at their final height, builders laid another row of stones over the inner edges of the walls, reaching into the interior of the building just slightly. Then came another layer and another, each reaching into the interior a bit more.

Eventually, the layers met in the center of the house to create a roof. Builders had to take great care, though. The roof could not be too large or it would collapse under its own weight. But built right, corbeled roofs were very strong and lasted for centuries.

A corbeled roof on a gate near the Maya city of Uxmal

ANCIENT SAUNAS

Ancient people enjoyed saunas as much as modern people do. In England, Russia, and other places, archaeologists have found piles of rocks that were probably used to heat ancient "sweat houses." Ancient people may have used saunas to keep themselves warm. Sick people probably used saunas for relief from fevers, arthritis, and other ailments. Sometimes saunas were used for religious ceremonies.

The ancient Maya were master sauna builders. Their sweat houses, called *temazcalli*, were probably built from stone. Heat came from a fire pit in the sauna floor or wall.

People sat on benches inside, throwing water onto glowing coals or hot stones to create steam. Temazcalli were still being used by the descendants of the Maya when Spanish conquerors arrived in Mexico in 1519.

The Mesoamerican civilizations declined long before the Spanish arrived. Eventually the ruins of their cities were covered by dense jungle undergrowth. Most people were unaware that previous civilizations had existed there until the mid-1800s, when ruins were uncovered.

ANCIENT GREECE

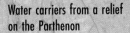

Water carriers from a relief
on the Parthenon

Mighty indeed are the marks and monuments in our empire which we have left," said Pericles, a leader of Athens in ancient Greece. "Future ages will wonder at us, as the present wonders at us now." Pericles was correct. Modern people still marvel at ancient Greek buildings and copy their designs.

Pericles lived from about 495 to 429 B.C. His home, Athens, was a great center of learning, art, and culture. One of its most famous sites was its acropolis, a group of temples, theaters, and government buildings set on a hill overlooking the city. Many Greek cities had acropolises. But the acropolis in Athens was so spectacular that it became known throughout the world as *The* Acropolis.

The Acropolis in Athens held some of the ancient world's most famous architecture. One building was the Parthenon, a temple honoring the goddess Athena. The Erechtheum was a shrine to Greek gods of agriculture. The Temple of Athena Nike was a symbol of harmony between Greek peoples. The Propylaea was a beautiful marble entranceway into the Acropolis itself.

TRICKING THE EYE

When seen from a distance, the Parthenon's marble columns and other architectural elements appear straight and perfectly proportioned. Actually, some of these elements were made deliberately out of proportion. Greek architects knew that perfectly even parts, when viewed from certain angles, create an optical illusion—they appear crooked and uneven.

The architects made the Parthenon's end columns a little thicker than its central columns, so that all appear equal from a distance. They spaced the end columns closer together than the central columns for the same reason. In addition, the Parthenon's base curves upward slightly—so that it appears flat from a distance.

The Parthenon stands on the Acropolis in Athens.

Ancient Wonders: Part 3

The Statue of Zeus at Olympia: The Statue of Zeus at Olympia, built around 450 B.C., honored the king of the Greek gods. The citizens of Olympia (the site of the ancient Olympic Games) had erected a magnificent temple to Zeus. But they had no suitable statue to put inside it. They asked a famous sculptor, Phidias, to make one.

Phidias had developed a new technique for making mammoth statues of gods and other characters. First he would build a wooden framework that outlined his subject's features. Then he covered the frame with sheets of metal and ivory to create the look of skin.

Phidias's statue at Olympia, 43 feet high, had Zeus sitting inside his temple on a marvelous throne inlaid with precious stones. The design was very clever. Zeus looked like he was about to stand up and smash through the roof of the temple.

People came from all around the world to worship at the temple. Viewing platforms even enabled visitors to climb up and inspect the details of Zeus's face. "On his head is a sculpted wreath of olive sprays," the Greek writer Pausanias noted about the statue in the second century A.D. "In his right hand is a figure of Victory, made from ivory and gold. In his left hand, the scepter inlaid with all metals, and an eagle perched on the scepter. The sandals of the god are made of gold, as is his robe."

In A.D. 40, the Roman emperor Caligula ordered workers to move the statue to Rome. Legend says that when they tried to raise it, Zeus let out a tremendous bellow that scared the workers away. The truth, historians say, is that the workers' scaffolding collapsed, and they gave up trying to move the statue.

The Temple of Artemis at Ephesus: The Temple of Artemis at Ephesus was called the most beautiful structure on earth. It honored Artemis, the Greek goddess of hunting and nature, whom the Romans called Diana.

King Croesus of Lydia ordered construction of the temple around 550 B.C. A Greek architect named Chersiphron designed it. It was the first major temple built from marble and was sometimes called "the Great Marble Temple." It rose from a large platform that overlooked a beautiful courtyard. Its roof was supported by 127 marble columns, each 66 feet high, perfectly aligned in rows. Inside was a large statue of Artemis.

People used the temple not just as a place of worship but also as a marketplace. The original temple was partly destroyed by fire in 356 B.C. It was rebuilt, but it burned again in A.D. 262.

The Colossus of Rhodes: The Colossus of Rhodes, a big statue of Helios, the sun god, stood in the Greek port city of Rhodes on the Aegean Sea. A sculptor named Chares of Lindos designed the colossus. Construction began in 294 B.C. and lasted 12 years. The statue was made out of an iron framework covered with sheets of bronze. Workers built from the ground up, filling the statue's legs with stones to keep it from tipping over. By building a spiral earthen ramp around the statue as they worked, laborers were able to reach the figure's upper portions.

The completed colossus was enormous, 110 feet high. "Few people can make their arms meet round the [figure's] thumb," wrote Pliny, a Roman historian.

The statue stood for only about 50 years. An earthquake toppled it in 226 B.C., leaving just the knees and lower legs standing. People came to see the wreckage for 900 more years, however.

In A.D. 654, Syrian soldiers conquered Rhodes and stripped away the statue's remaining bronze skin. Nine hundred camels carried the bronze back to Syria, where it was probably melted to make coins.

The Pharos of Alexandria: The Pharos of Alexandria was a lighthouse located on the island of Pharos in the Mediterranean Sea. It was the world's first lighthouse, and it guided many ships past reefs and safely into the harbor of Alexandria.

The lighthouse consisted of three huge marble towers, built one on top of the other to a total height of 384 feet. The structure was topped by a statue of Zeus, king of the Greek gods. Construction began around 290 B.C. and lasted 20 years.

Inside the lighthouse, workers climbed a ramp to deliver fuel for the fire that guided ships. The fire burned at night in front of a polished bronze reflector. Its light could be seen for 30 miles. In daytime the reflector gleamed with the light of the sun.

Strong earthquakes in A.D. 1303 and 1323 seriously damaged the Pharos. Within 25 years it was reduced to ruins. By 1480, when Egyptians built a fort on the site, the lighthouse was completely gone. But the Pharos lived on. It became a model for lighthouses around the world. The French sculptor Frédéric-Auguste Bartholdi used it as the model for the Statue of Liberty in New York City. And look up the word *lighthouse* in a Spanish, Italian, or French dictionary, and you'll see that the name Pharos lives on as well.

COPYCAT ARCHITECTURE: THE LINCOLN MEMORIAL

American architect Henry Bacon, who lived from 1866 to 1924, loved the Parthenon. He studied its design carefully and used it as a model for his most famous structure, the Lincoln Memorial in Washington, D.C.

The memorial, built between 1915 and 1922, has a base of stone steps leading to an open chamber containing a 19-foot statue of President Abraham Lincoln. The building has 36 marble columns, each 44 feet high.

GREEK COLUMNS

No part of ancient Greek architecture is more classically "Greek" than the long rows of marble columns found in temples. The Temple of Artemis at Ephesus, one of the Seven Wonders of the Ancient World, had 127 columns that were lined up in perfect rows. Historians often say that such orderly columns reflect the order and harmony of Greek society. But the Greeks used lots of columns for another reason. They had to build structures with lots of columns or their roofs would have fallen down!

Many Greek structures were made mostly of stone. Roofs and doorways were made of stone slabs laid across the tops of stone columns. Without enough support, stone can be very weak. In fact, a long stone slab will break under its own weight unless supported by a lot of columns. So while the columns in Greek buildings might look elegant, they also have another, more practical purpose.

There were three basic orders, or styles, of Greek columns: Doric, Ionic, and Corinthian. Each kind of column had a long shaft and top and bottom elements carved and decorated in a specific way.

The capitals (tops) of two kinds of Greek columns, Ionic (left) and Corinthian (right)

Greek architects often followed standard formulas when building temples. The formulas told architects what kind and how many columns to use in a temple, how big the columns should be, and how much space to leave between them. One popular temple style had a row of Doric columns around the building and six columns out front. Despite the formulas, Greek architects could still use their own creativity in designing the details of temples and other buildings.

As structures became more complex in ancient Greece, building became more of a science. Builders also had to be mathematicians and engineers who could calculate exactly how much weight a slab of stone could bear before cracking.

They had to space columns correctly. If the columns were placed too far apart, the stone slabs bridging the gaps between the columns would crack. If columns were too close together, money would be wasted on unneeded columns, which were very expensive to carve and assemble.

A BEAUTIFUL TOWN

One of the most famous planned cities in ancient times was Alexandria, built in 331 B.C. in an area of Egypt that had been conquered by Greece. A Greek architect named Dinocrates planned the city, with seven broad streets running parallel to the Mediterranean coast. Eleven other streets intersected these seven at right angles. The longest street, the Canopic, was about 3.5 miles long. Another long road, the Heptastadion, connected Alexandria to the famous Pharos, or lighthouse, that guarded its harbor.

Alexandria and some other Greek towns had beautiful terraces. Archaeologists think that the idea for terraces, and the technology for building them, probably filtered down from Mesopotamia to Egypt to Greece.

7

ANCIENT ROME

The Romans built bigger and stronger structures than any other ancient civilization. How did they do it? By borrowing construction technology from neighboring peoples and then improving on it. From the Greeks, the Romans borrowed the idea of magnificent public buildings. From the Etruscans, they borrowed the arch. The Romans also introduced an important construction technology of their own. It was concrete. With concrete the Romans were able to build huge domes, long bridges—even a giant stadium.

RAISING THE ROOF

An arch is a curved structure used to span an opening, such as a window or doorway. Even a whole room or building can be covered by an arched roof. The Romans were the first ancient people to make widespread use of the arch in buildings and other structures.

Arches are strong. Unlike the flat stone slabs used above doorways and walls in Greek temples, arches won't collapse under their own weight. With arches, Roman builders could cover open spaces without using long rows of stone columns underneath.

The simplest arches cover doorways and windows. But Roman builders expanded on the arch idea to create the vault, a roof or ceiling resembling a soda can cut in half lengthwise. The dome, also based on the arch design, is a roof that looks like a basketball cut in half.

BUILDING BETTER BRIDGES

The Romans realized that arches were perfect for building strong bridges. In an arched bridge, the curved, upper part of the arch supports the roadway over a river. The two legs resting on the riverbanks carry the load.

The Romans built arched bridges throughout their empire. A single arch could span a small river. To make longer bridges, Roman engineers laid several arches end-to-end across rivers. Underwater supports kept the legs of the inner arches—those in the middle of a river—from sinking into the soft mud of the river bottom. Some ancient Roman bridges are still standing. Some are even in everyday use!

ONE LARGE POZZOLANA WITH PEPPERONI?

Don't even think of eating pozzolana. Pozzolana is volcanic ash that comes from the Italian city of Pozzuoli. The reddish brown ash contains chemicals that make it a wonderful natural cement. By mixing pozzolana with lime and crushed stone, ancient Roman builders made a totally new material—concrete. Pozzolana mixed with pumice, a light volcanic glass, made a very lightweight concrete.

Built in 17 B.C., the Pantheon has an enormous concrete dome.

Concrete revolutionized building in ancient Rome. It made construction faster, easier, and cheaper. For instance, Roman workers could quickly pour concrete walls that would have taken years to build from brick.

First, builders made hollow wooden forms, which were filled with concrete. When the concrete hardened, workers tore down the forms. This method allowed builders to create architectural elements never before possible, including domes for roofs. The Pantheon, a famous Roman temple, had a huge concrete dome that was 142 feet in diameter.

ANCIENT SUPERDOME

The Romans also used concrete to build the Colosseum, a giant amphitheater—the biggest in the world for some 1,900 years. Built in Rome between A.D. 70 and 80, the Colosseum was 620 feet long and 513 feet wide. While other ancient amphitheaters were dug into cliffs or hillsides, the Colosseum was freestanding. Its sturdy concrete walls could stand alone without outside support.

The Colosseum seated 50,000 spectators—more than some modern football stadiums. From its marble seats, spectators watched fights between gladiators and between gladiators and wild animals. Sometimes the Colosseum was even flooded for mock battles between ships.

BIG CITY, BIG BUILDINGS

Rome's population reached about 1.5 million at the peak of the Roman Empire. In addition to a big population, the city also had very tall buildings—some more than six stories. The poet Juvenal, writing in the first century A.D., said that some Roman buildings were so high that people looking out windows had trouble seeing carts on the streets below. Architects tried to outdo each other by creating taller and taller buildings.

The emperor Augustus, who lived from 63 B.C. to A.D. 14, worried that the tall buildings were spoiling Rome's appearance. He issued a decree forbidding the construction of buildings higher than 60 feet—about six stories.

LET THE LIGHT SHINE IN

Window glass was one of the greatest advances in construction technology. Imagine living, as people did for thousands of years, in a home without windows—or a home with windows, but no window glass. Yes, windows without glass let in light. But they also let in cold air, insects, birds, wind, rain, and snow.

Historians believe that the ancient Egyptians discovered how to make glass out of sand and other materials more than 5,600 years ago. By 1500 B.C., the Phoenicians had become master glassmakers. They exported beautiful glass vases, bowls, and other objects around the Mediterranean world.

The Phoenicians also perfected the art of glassblowing, which involved shaping molten glass by blowing through a tube. The first window glass was probably made from a bubble of blown glass, opened into a flat sheet.

Roman glassmakers borrowed and improved upon the glassmaking technology of the Phoenicians. Before Roman glassmaking, only the rich could afford glass. But by the first century B.C., window glass had grown less expensive. It became common in many Roman towns, especially in the north, where the weather was cool.

The Romans probably made window glass by casting—pouring molten glass into smooth molds. Most window-panes were about 12 by 24 inches, although some were much bigger. One windowpane from Pompeii was 40 inches long, 28 inches wide, and a half-inch thick.

160 NORTH STREET

Many Roman towns started out as military camps, and all were based on the same pattern. Usually two main streets crossed in the town center, dividing the town into four quarters. The main streets were usually named according to the points on a compass—north, south, east, and west. Smaller streets led off the main streets.

Many modern towns are based on the Roman system— divided into four "quarters." New Orleans, with its French Quarter, is an example. Many modern streets also have north, south, east, and west designations, just like streets in ancient Rome.

BUILT TO LAST

Fifty thousand miles of roads connected parts of the Roman Empire. The oldest and most famous road was the Via Appia, or Appian Way. Leading from Rome to Italy's southeast coast, the road was more than 350 miles long, 35 feet wide, and very straight. A general named Appius Claudius began construction on the road in 312 B.C.

Roman roads were engineered to last. Each had a sturdy foundation, up to five feet thick, made of packed earth and layers of stone blocks, broken stone, sand, and other material. Roads were paved with blocks of cut stone.

Roads through rainy areas had cambered, or arched, sur- faces—higher in the center than at the sides. This shape let rainwater drain off quickly, so that it didn't soak in and damage the pavement. Most Roman roads also had curb- stones and drainage ditches at the sides.

Roman roads remained the best in Europe for centuries, long after the fall of the Roman Empire. The Via Appia was so well built that parts of it are still in use!

WATERWORKS

An aqueduct is a structure for carrying a large amount of flowing water. People in ancient Mesopotamia built the first aqueducts, but the Romans were the ancient world's greatest aqueduct builders. Between 312 B.C. and A.D. 226, Roman engineers built 11 aqueducts. Some of them were bridgelike structures that brought water across valleys. Other aqueducts were underground pipes.

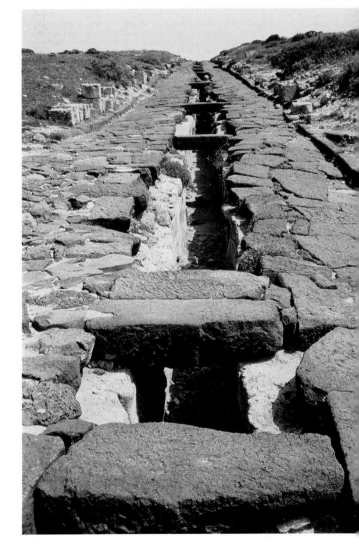

This Roman road on the island of Sardinia had an underground water channel.

From mountain streams and springs, the aqueducts brought about 97 million gallons of water to Rome each day, over distances as far as 57 miles. The total system covered 260 miles. Water flowed into big distribution tanks, then through more pipes into buildings, fountains, toilets, and sewers.

BATHS AND TOILETS

The ancient Romans washed at public bathhouses and used public toilets. These were very public bathrooms indeed—consisting of a series of stone toilets running along walls in busy sections of town. Each toilet had an opening where the user sat. A drainage system carried waste into a sewer.

Some Roman bathrooms could accommodate 15 or 20 people at the same time. The Romans did not find this lack of privacy embarrassing. It was their custom to chat with one another while they "went about their business."

ANOTHER GREAT TUNNEL

If you think the pedestrian tunnel in ancient Babylon was impressive, wait until you hear about a tunnel built in A.D. 41 in ancient Rome. It was 3.5 miles long. It took 30,000 workers 10 years to build. The tunnel drained water from Lake Fucinus to make acres of new farmland.

To create the tunnel, workers dug shafts about 120 feet apart and 400 feet deep. Climbing ladders down to the bottom of each shaft, workers then dug sideways until they met, connecting the tunnel from one shaft to the next.

How did the Romans and other ancient builders dig big tunnels without drills and other power tools? You might think they dug through soft rock. Surprisingly, ancient

A twelve-seat bathroom at a public bathhouse in Tunisia, part of the early Roman Empire

builders preferred to dig tunnels through very hard rock. In hard rock, tunnel walls would stand up without special supports or linings of brick or stone.

Actually, tunnel builders usually didn't dig rock, they burned it. They used a technique called fire-quenching—heating the rock with fire, then cooling it quickly with water. The fast cooling process caused the rock to crack, making it easy to remove. Workers hauled away the rock, built another fire, and kept up the process as a tunnel grew foot by foot.

COPYCAT ARCHITECTURE: THE RENAISSANCE

The Renaissance, which began in the 1300s, was a period of European history marked by new learning, literature, art, and architecture. *Renaissance* means "rebirth," and architects of this period were very interested in reviving the styles of ancient Greece and Rome. Architects began copying ancient structures, often using domes, vaults, Corinthian columns, and other features straight out of Greece and Rome.

Why were people so interested in ancient building styles? One big reason was the discovery of a handbook for Roman architects, written by Marcus Vitruvius Pollio around 27 B.C. The guide, *De Architectura*—"On Architecture"—dealt with all aspects of architecture, including building materials, flooring, construction of temples and other public buildings, and even the education of architects.

An architect's work was so important, Vitruvius wrote, that he "should be a man of letters, a skilled draughtsman, a mathematician, familiar with historical studies, a diligent student of philosophy, acquainted with music, not ignorant of medicine." Vitruvius offered this advice on town planning:

In setting out the walls of a city, the choice of a healthy situation is of the first importance. It should be on high ground, neither subject to fogs nor rains. Its aspects should be neither violently hot nor intensely cold, but temperate in both respects. The neighborhood of a marshy place must be avoided.

De Architectura was the most important book of its kind for hundreds of years. European architects during the 1600s, 1700s, and 1800s included many of its ideas in their own books on architecture.

COPYCAT ARCHITECTURE: NEOCLASSICISM

Another wave of interest in the architecture of ancient Greece and Rome occurred in Europe in the mid-1700s. This wave started after archaeologists began to excavate the ancient Roman cities of Pompeii and Herculaneum. Both cities had been buried for over a thousand years under a thick layer of volcanic ash from the eruption of Mount Vesuvius in A.D. 79.

Architects copied the designs of the buildings that were uncovered by the excavations and were able to reproduce ancient styles much more closely than architects of the Renaissance. The new building style was called neoclassical—*neo* means "new," and *classical* refers to the culture and art of ancient Greece and Rome.

AFTER THE ANCIENTS

When ancient times ended with the collapse of the Roman Empire in A.D. 476, a lot of ancient construction technology was forgotten. Many centuries passed before people were able to create buildings that equaled the ancient structures in size, strength, and design. Modern architects still copy classical Greek and Roman architecture and regard ancient structures as among the greatest ever built. When historians make up lists of the most marvelous buildings ever erected, they always include the Seven Wonders of the Ancient World.

The Panthéon in Paris, France, was built in the mid- to late 1700s in the neoclassical style.

The modern world includes many great buildings too. In fact, architects have named the "Wonders of the Modern World," including the Channel Tunnel, Big Ben in London, the Eiffel Tower in Paris, the Empire State Building in New

York City, the Gateway Arch in St. Louis, Missouri, the Golden Gate Bridge in San Francisco, the High Dam in Aswan, Egypt, and the Hoover Dam in Nevada. Are these structures as wondrous as the seven ancient wonders? When you consider that the ancient builders made their giant monuments without cranes, trucks, bulldozers, elevators, and other powerful machinery, there's really no comparison!

GLOSSARY

acropolis—a fortified section of an ancient Greek city, containing temples and government buildings and located on a hill

aqueduct—a structure, such as a canal or pipe, for carrying a large amount of flowing water

arch—a curved architectural structure that is used to span an opening, such as a doorway

archaeologist—a scientist who studies the remains of past human cultures

architecture—the art and science of designing and building structures

bitumen—a by-product of petroleum, used as cement and mortar in ancient times

corbeled roof—a roof made of layers of stones or other material. Each successive layer projects farther into the interior of the building than the last, until the two sides of the roof meet.

dome—a large hemispherical (resembling half a ball) roof or ceiling

mud and wattle—a method of building homes using a framework of poles or reeds covered by mud

suspension bridge—a bridge hung from cables that are strung over a river or valley

terrace—a raised mound of earth or a series of ledges cut into a hillside

thatch—a mat of straw or other plant material used as a roof

vault—an arched roof that resembles a barrel or tunnel

SELECTED BIBLIOGRAPHY

Adkins, Lesley, and Roy A. Adkins. *Handbook to Life in Ancient Rome.* New York: Facts on File, 1994.

Clark, Ronald W. *Works of Man.* New York: Viking, 1985.

Courtenay-Thompson, Fiona, Roger Tritton, and Nicola Liddiard, eds. *The Visual Dictionary of Buildings.* London: Dorling Kindersley, 1992.

Cox, Reg, and Neil Morris. *The Seven Wonders of the Ancient World.* Parsippany, N.J.: Silver Burdett Press, 1996.

Ingpen, Robert, and Philip Wilkinson. *Encyclopedia of Ideas That Changed the World.* New York: Penguin Books, 1993.

James, Peter, and Nick Thorpe. *Ancient Inventions.* New York: Ballantine Books, 1994.

Oates, David, and Joan Oates. *The Rise of Civilization.* New York: Elsevier Phaidon, 1976.

Raeburn, Michael. *Architecture of the World.* New York: Galahad Books, 1975.

Saggs, H. W. F. *Civilization Before Greece and Rome.* New Haven, Conn.: Yale University Press, 1989.

Stevenson, Neil. *Architecture.* New York: Dorling Kindersley, 1997.

White, K. D. *Greek and Roman Technology.* Ithaca, N.Y.: Cornell University Press, 1984.

INDEX

ABOUT THE AUTHORS

Michael Woods is an award-winning science and medical writer with the Washington bureau of the *Toledo Blade* and the *Pittsburgh Post Gazette.* His articles and weekly health column, "The Medical Journal," appear in newspapers around the United States. Born in Dunkirk, New York, Mr. Woods developed a love for science and writing in childhood and studied both topics in school. His many awards include an honorary doctorate degree for helping to develop the profession of science writing. His previous work includes a children's book on Antarctica, where he has traveled on three expeditions.

Mary B. Woods is an elementary school librarian in the Fairfax County, Virginia, public school system. Born in New Rochelle, New York, Mrs. Woods studied history in college and later received a master's degree in library science. She is coauthor of a children's book on new discoveries about the ancient Maya civilization.

Photo Acknowledgments: The photographs in this book are reproduced courtesy of: © Ruggero Vanni/Corbis, p. 1; Erich Lessing/Art Resource, NY, pp. 2–3, 19, 20–21, 24, 39, 46, 57, 59, 60–61, 65, 69, 73; © Charles O'Rear/Corbis, p. 11; Caves of Lascaux, Dordogne, France/Bridgeman Art Library, pp. 12–13; © Hubert Stadler/Corbis, p. 16; © Roger Ressmeyer/Corbis, p. 17; Choga Zambil (ancient Al-Untash), Iran/Bridgeman Art Library, p. 23; Iraq Museum, Baghdad, Iraq/Bridgeman Art Library, p. 28; © Werner Forman/Art Resource, NY, p. 31; © The Purcell Team/Corbis, p. 33; Private Collection/Bridgeman Art Library, pp. 34–35; © Kenneth Garrett, p. 37; © Pierre Colombel/Corbis, p. 41; National Museum of India, New Delhi, India/Bridgeman Art Library, pp. 42–43; © Diego Lezama Orezzoli/Corbis, p. 44; The Great Wall, China/Bridgeman Art Library, p. 49; © Danny Leham/Corbis, p. 51; © Charles and Josette Lenars/Corbis, pp. 52–53; © Gian Berto Vanni/Corbis, p. 55; © Jim Winkley/Ecosce/Corbis, p. 62; SEF/Art Resource, p. 67 (both); © Mimmo Jodice/Corbis, pp. 70–71; Tharros, Sardinia, Italy/INDEX/Bridgeman Art Library, p. 77; © Roger Wood/Corbis, p. 79; Giraudon/Art Resource, p. 82.

Front cover photographs courtesy of: © Kenneth Garrett *(upper left and upper right)* and Eric Lessing/Art Resource, NY *(lower left).*